Contents

Heavy or Light?

Color, cut, and paste. Show which things are **heavy** and which things are **light**.

 light

 heavy

Cool, Man, Cool!

The tortoise wants to look cool. Can you color its shell in a special way? Add shoes and a hat.

Tell what the tortoise looks like.

_____

_____.

In a Shell

Draw another animal that lives in a shell.
Draw the place where it lives, too.

I am a _____ .

I live _____

_____

_____ .

Put It in the Pack

I'm going on a camping trip.
I will put the things
I need in my pack.

I'll need socks.

I'll need a shirt.

I'll need shorts.

I'll need a sweatshirt.

Put it in the pack.

I'll need a hat.

I'll need food.

I'll need my sleeping bag.

I'll need a flashlight.

I'll need Teddy.

Put me in the pack!

I'll put the pack on my back.
Help! I can't move.

I can't hike to the camp.
I'll take out a few things.

I don't have to have socks.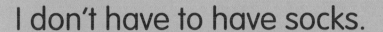

I don't have to have a shirt.

I don't have to have shorts.

I don't have to have a sweatshirt.

I don't have to have a hat.

I don't have to have food.

I don't have to have a sleeping bag.

I don't have to have a flashlight.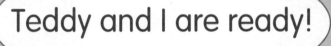

Teddy and I are ready!

Let's go!

After You Read

Practice reading this page. When you can read it with no mistakes, read it tio an adult.

What Did It Say?

Fill in a circle to answer each question.

1. Where is the little girl going?

   ○   ○   ○

2. How will the little girl carry her things?

   ○   ○   ○

3. What is the little girl's problem?

   ○   ○   ○

4. What does the little girl take out that she will need?

   ○   ○   ○

Reading • EMC 4529 • © Evan-Moor Corp.

Connect the Dots

Start with 1. Make something you might see on a camping trip.

Make a list of animals you might see on a camping trip.

_____   _____   _____

_____   _____   _____

An Ant on the Rug

There's an ant on the rug, on the rug.
There's an ant on the rug, on the rug.
What a tiny bug, little ant on the rug.
There's an ant on the rug, on the rug.

There's an ant on my toe, on my toe.
There's an ant on my toe, on my toe.
Where will it go, that ant on my toe?
There's an ant on my toe, on my toe.

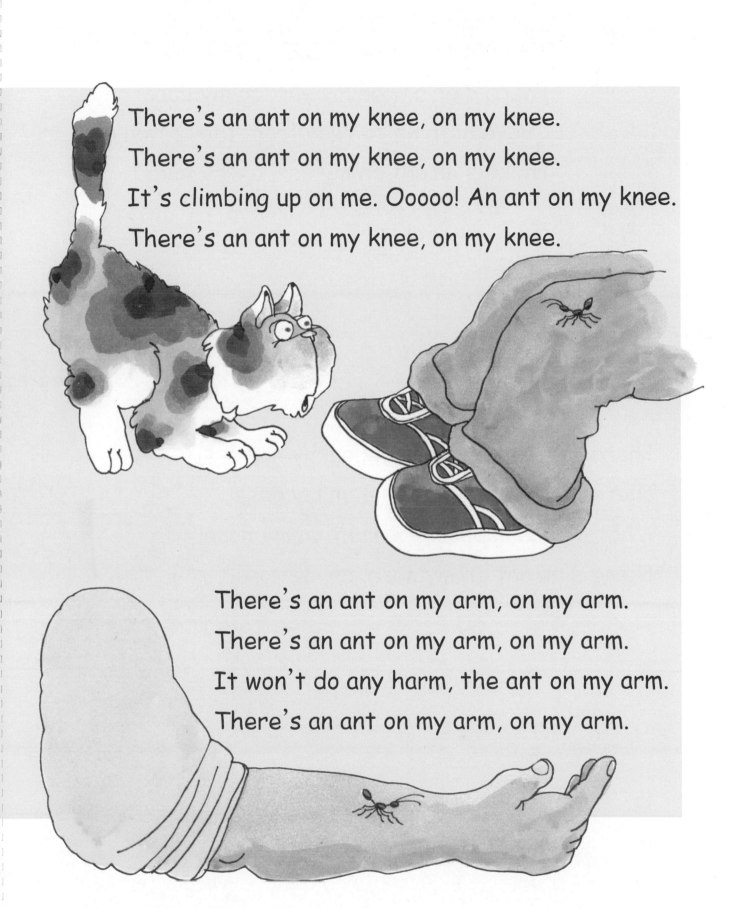

There's an ant on my knee, on my knee.

There's an ant on my knee, on my knee.

It's climbing up on me. Ooooo! An ant on my knee.

There's an ant on my knee, on my knee.

There's an ant on my arm, on my arm.

There's an ant on my arm, on my arm.

It won't do any harm, the ant on my arm.

There's an ant on my arm, on my arm.

There's an ant on my ear, on my ear.

There's an ant on my ear, on my ear.

I have nothing to fear from the ant on my ear.

There's an ant on my ear, on my ear.

There's an ant on my nose, on my nose.

There's an ant on my nose, on my nose.

What do you suppose? An ant on my nose!

There's an ant on my nose, on my nose.

There's an ant in my hair, in my hair.

There's an ant in my hair, in my hair.

I am very aware there's an ant in my hair.

There's an ant in my hair, in my hair.

There's an ant in a jar, in a jar.

There's an ant in a jar, in a jar.

It traveled near and far,

　but now it's in a jar.

There's an ant in a jar, in a jar.

After You Read

Practice your favorite part of the story. When you can read it quickly, read it to an adult.

What Did It Say?

Draw a line to show where the ant was.

First

Next

Next

Next

Next

Next

Next

At the end

Do you think the boy was happy to have the ant in the jar?

yes   no

Why do you think the way you do?

_____

_____

Working with Word Families

ug

r + ug = __ __ __   b + ug = __ __ __

d + ug = __ __ __   h + ug = __ __ __

pl + ug = __ __ __ __   sn + ug = __ __ __ __

Use the new words to complete these sentences.

Be careful when you

touch the _____.

Look at the hole

I _____.

Dad gave me

a _____.

He's as _____ as a

_____ in a _____.

Same Sound

Color the pictures that have the same ⓐ sound as 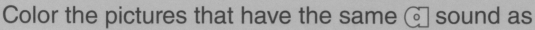 .

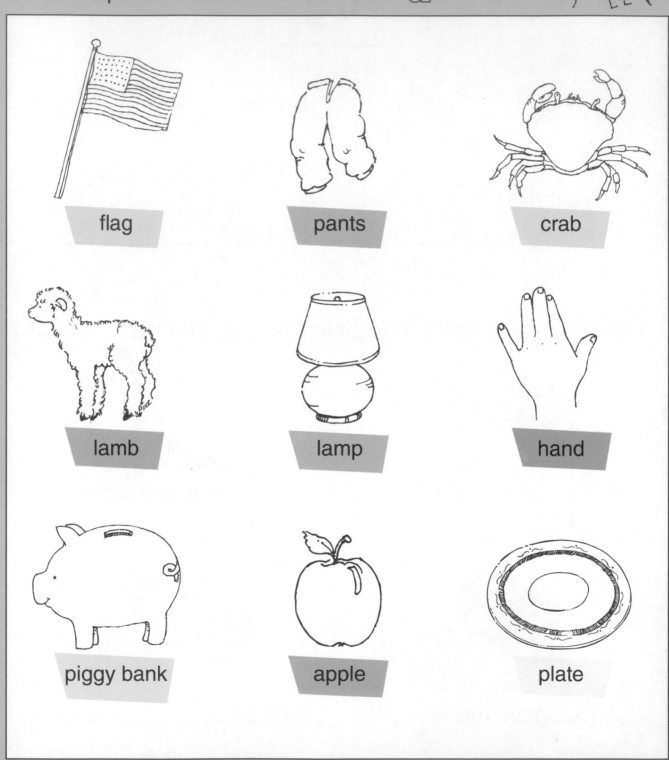

flag	pants	crab
lamb	lamp	hand
piggy bank	apple	plate

Reading • EMC 4529 • © Evan-Moor Corp.

What Does It Mean?

Cut and paste to label the picture.

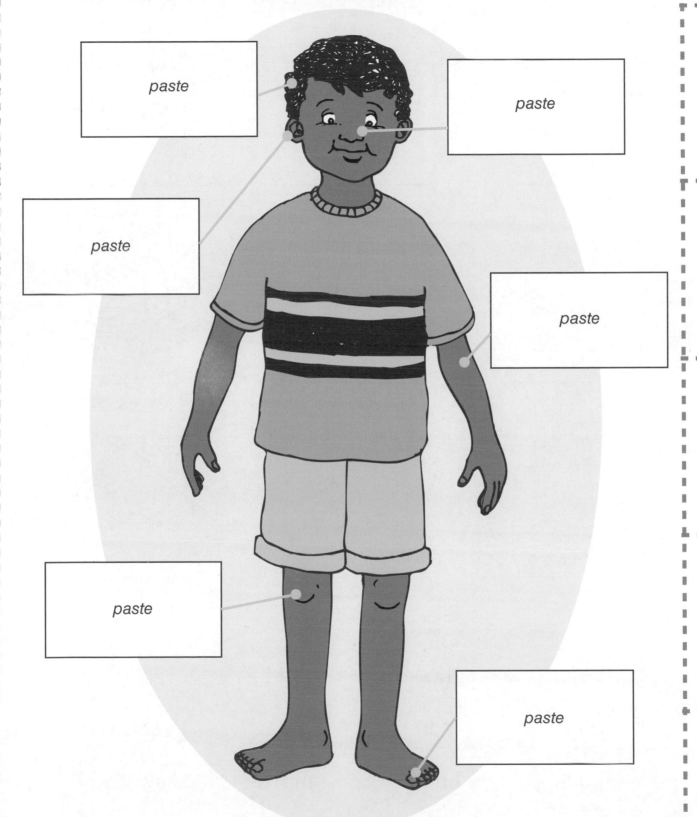

paste

paste

paste

paste

paste

paste

hair

nose

ear

arm

knee

toe

Rhyme Time

Color the pictures in each row that rhyme.
Write the words under the pictures.

 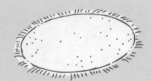 

_____ _____ _____

_____ _____ _____

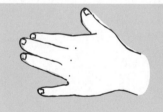  

_____ _____ _____

bell	flag	hen	rug
bug	fan	pen	sand
car	hand	plate	skate

Who Lives in the Barn?

Cut out the flaps on the other side of this page.
Paste them on the story pages to make a flap book.

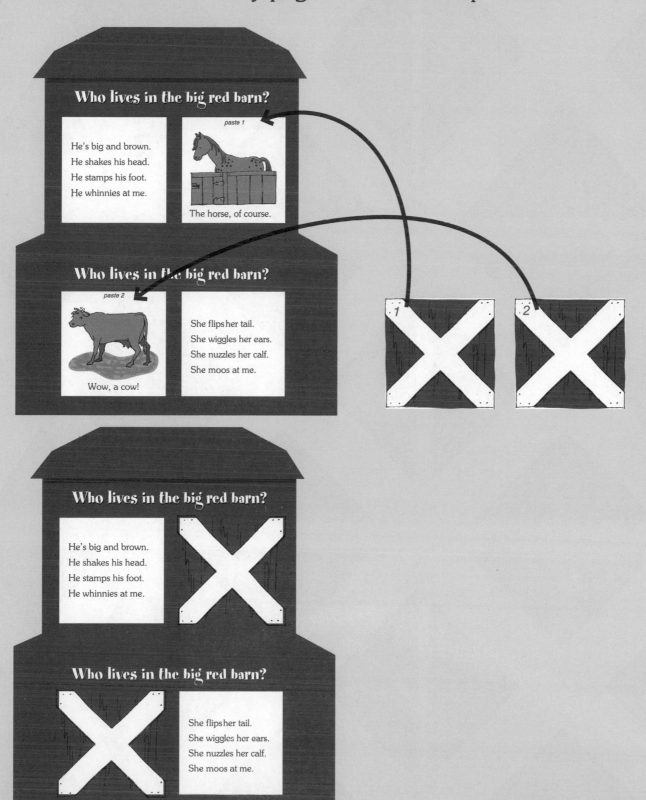

Who lives in the big red barn?

He's big and brown.
He shakes his head.
He stamps his foot.
He whinnies at me.

paste 1

The horse, of course.

Who lives in the big red barn?

paste 2

Wow, a cow!

She flips her tail.
She wiggles her ears.
She nuzzles her calf.
She moos at me.

1

2

Who lives in the big red barn?

He's big and brown.
He shakes his head.
He stamps his foot.
He whinnies at me.

Who lives in the big red barn?

She flips her tail.
She wiggles her ears.
She nuzzles her calf.
She moos at me.

54

Who lives in the big red barn?

He's big and brown.

He shakes his head.

He stamps his foot.

He whinnies at me.

paste 1

The horse, of course.

Who lives in the big red barn?

paste 2

Wow, a cow!

She flips her tail.

She wiggles her ears.

She nuzzles her calf.

She moos at me.

Who lives in the big red barn?

She wears her winter coat.

She has a little bell.

She wakes her lamb.

She baas at me.

paste 3

My sheep's asleep.

Who lives in the big red barn?

paste 4

*Let's follow
the swallow.*

It flies from the roof.

It builds a small nest.

It sits on its eggs.

It peeps at me.

Who lives in the big red barn?

He stands by the door.

He runs to me.

He licks my hand.

He barks at me.

paste 5

Not a frog! It's my dog.

Who lives in the big red barn?

She laps the milk.

She licks her paws.

She feeds her kittens.

She purrs at me.

paste 6

*Mother cat!
Think of that.*

Who lives in the big red barn?

It runs so fast.

It hides so well.

It nibbles food.

It squeaks at me.

paste 7

The barn is a house for the mouse.

Who lives in the big red barn?

paste 8

A horse,
A cow,
A sheep,
A swallow,
A dog,
A cat,
And a mouse.
That's who!

paste 9

What Did It Say?

Fill in the circle under the correct answer.

1. Who builds a small nest?

sheep	swallow	cat	mouse
○	○	○	○

2. Who nibbles food?

sheep	swallow	cat	mouse
○	○	○	○

3. Who has a lamb?

sheep	swallow	cat	mouse
○	○	○	○

4. Who flips her tail?

horse	cow	dog	cat
○	○	○	○

5. Who licks a paw?

horse	cow	dog	cat
○	○	○	○

6. Who barks?

horse	cow	dog	cat
○	○	○	○

7. Who stamps a foot?

horse	cow	dog	cat
○	○	○	○

Working with Word Families

ake

c + ake = __ __ __ __   sn + ake = __ __ __ __ __

r + ake = __ __ __ __   sh + ake = __ __ __ __ __

fl + ake = __ __ __ __ __   br + ake = __ __ __ __ __

Write the correct **-ake** word to finish each sentence.
Draw a picture to show what the sentence says.

I _____ up the leaves.

A _____ of snow is on my nose.

Which Came First?

Cut and paste to put the animals in order.
Use the rhyme to help.

Who lives in the barn?

The [*paste*] , of course.

Wow, a [*paste*] !

My [*paste*] is asleep.

Let's follow the [*paste*] .

Not a frog! It's my [*paste*] .

Think of that, Mother [*paste*] !

The barn is a house for the [*paste*] .

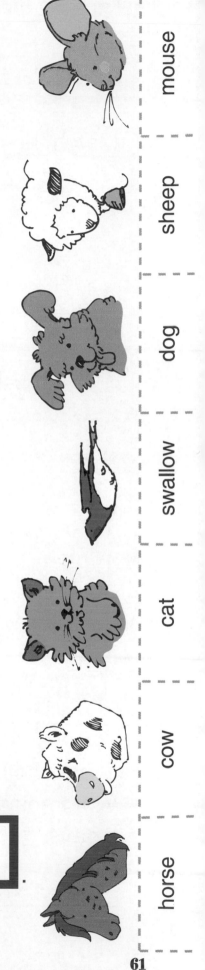

mouse

sheep

dog

swallow

cat

cow

horse

What Does It Say?

Match the noise word to the animal that makes that noise.

baa

whinny

purr

squeak

chirp

moo

woof

Draw another animal here.
What noise does it make?
It says

_____.

Think About It

Which animals live mainly on a farm?
Which animals live mainly in the jungle?
Write the names of the animals in the correct list.

goat   lion   elephant   chicken

horse   zebra   cow   monkey

 On a farm    In the jungle

_____   _____

_____   _____

_____   _____

_____   _____

The Big Red Barn

Read the color words. Then color the picture.

The Fix-It Man

Hello, Mr. Fix-It.
Could you come to my house?

The fix-it man came to my house.
He fixed the stove.

Reading • EMC 4529 • © Evan-Moor Corp.

The fix-it man came to my house.
He fixed the door.

Hello, Mr. Fix-It. Please come fast.

The fix-it man came to my house.
We had cookies and milk.

What Did It Say?

Fill in the circle by the correct answer.

1. Who did the boy call for help?
   ○ Mother   ○ a friend   ○ Mr. Fix-It

2. What was wrong with the window?
   ○ It was stuck.   ○ It broke.   ○ It needed washing.

3. Was Mr. Fix-It a good fixer?
   ○ No, he had to keep coming back.
   ○ Yes, he won a prize.
   ○ Yes, he fixed everything.

4. Why do you think the boy called Mr. Fix-It the last time?
   ○ There were too many cookies in the jar.
   ○ The milk was going to spoil.
   ○ Mr. Fix-It should have a treat.

Write an answer.
Who fixes things at your house?

_____

_____

_____

Put It in Order

Mr. Fix-It will fix the wagon. Color the pictures.
Cut and paste to put them in the correct order.

1

paste

2

paste

3

paste

4

paste

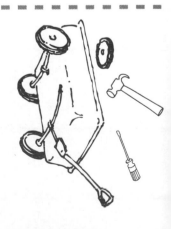

71

Can It Be Fixed?

Some things cannot be put back together.
Write It can be fixed or It can't by each
of the pictures below. Use your best
handwriting.

It can't

_____

_____

_____

_____

_____

Working with Word Families

ink

p + ink = _ _ _ _

s + ink = _ _ _ _

bl + ink = _ _ _ _ _

dr + ink = _ _ _ _ _

shr + ink = _ _ _ _ _ _

th + ink = _ _ _ _ _

Draw a toy boat in a sink.	Draw a muddy pig that's pink.

More Than One

Add **s** to each word to mean **more than one**.
Then draw what the words say.

one door

two _____

one house

three _____

one bird

four _____

one flower

five _____

Rhyme Time

Color the pictures. Circle the words that rhyme.

house	mouse	cat
window	sink	ink
door	bear	chair
dish	milk	fish
cake	snake	hat

What a

Monday
I have muffins.
Munch! Munch!

Tuesday
I have tuna.
Tasty!

Wednesday
I have waffles.
Wow!

Thursday
I have Thanksgiving turkey.
Thanks!

M
T
W
Th

Week!

Friday
I have fries.
Free fries!

Saturday
I have sodas.
Sip it!

Sunday
I have soup.
See it simmer.

Ummmm—What can I eat next week?

What Did I Have?

Fill in the circle under the correct answer.

1. What did I have on Tuesday?

turkey   tuna   soup
○   ○   ○

2. What did I have on Friday?

waffles   muffins   fries
○   ○   ○

3. What did I have on Sunday?

soup   soda   turkey
○   ○   ○

4. What did I have on Monday?

waffles   fries   muffins
○   ○   ○

5. What did I have on Saturday?

soup   soda   tuna
○   ○   ○

My Favorite Foods

Rewrite the story. Draw or write what you would like to eat each day. Then read the story using your foods.

Monday
I have

Tuesday
I have

Wednesday
I have

Thursday
I have

Friday
I have

Saturday
I have

Sunday
I have

Working with Word Families

unch

l + unch = __ __ __ __ __   m + unch = __ __ __ __ __

b + unch = __ __ __ __ __   p + unch = __ __ __ __ __

cr + unch = __ __ __ __ __ __

Circle each word from the **-unch** family in the story below.
Draw pictures to show the animals eating.

See the goats? They like to eat. Munch, munch, Hay for lunch.	See the squirrels? They like to eat. Munch, munch, Hear the crunch.	See the monkeys? They like to eat. Munch, munch, What a bunch!

Noisy Foods

Some foods are noisy. Color the things that make crunchy noises when you eat them. Write **munch** under the ones you like to eat.

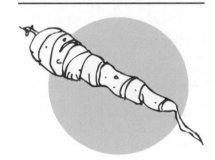

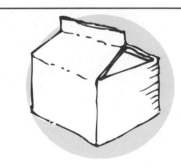

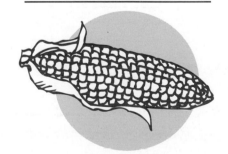

How Does It Taste?

Write one letter of the food name in each box. When all the boxes have been filled in, read the secret message in the pink boxes.

Foods

milk	apple	custard
fruit	cookie	bread
eggs	chocolate	pudding

Row 1: ☐ ☐ ☐ ☐ ☐ ☐ d

Row 2: ☐ ☐ ☐ a ☐

Row 3: ☐ p ☐ ☐ ☐

Row 4: f ☐ ☐ ☐ ☐

Row 5: ☐ ☐ ☐ k ☐ ☐

Row 6: ☐ i ☐ ☐

Row 7: ☐ h ☐ ☐ ☐ ☐ ☐ ☐

Row 8: p ☐ ☐ ☐ ☐ ☐

Row 9: ☐ g ☐ ☐

Write the secret message here: _____

Skills:Seeing the Whole

Food Word Search

See how many of the foods in the Word Box you can find.

Word Box

☐ apple   ☐ banana   ☐ spaghetti
☐ cookie   ☐ pizza   ☐ cheese
☐ grapes   ☐ pancake   ☑ hamburger
☐ orange   ☐ carrot   ☐ tuna
☐ potatoes   ☐ eggs   ☐ corn

```
h a m b u r g e r t w
a p p l e c a r p u p
n c g r a p e s i n o
c a t r u c k s z a t
o r c h e e s e z x a
o r j c o r n z a m t
k o p a n c a k e y o
i t r a b b i t u p e
e r b a n a n a x t s
p s p a g h e t t i z
o r a n g e w e g g s
```

© Evan-Moor Corp. • EMC 4529 • Reading

83

Molly and Max

This is Molly.

This is Max.

They played together all week.

Monday they played hide and seek.

Molly hid under the blanket.

Max hid behind the plant.

Reading • EMC 4529 • © Evan-Moor Corp.

Tuesday they dug holes in the yard.

Molly buried a bone.

Max picked some flowers.

Wednesday they went for a walk.

Molly walked and sniffed.

Max walked round and round.

Thursday they learned to open doors.

Molly went in and out.

Max found the trash.

Friday they practiced jumping.

Molly jumped high.

Max jumped too high.

Reading • EMC 4529 • © Evan-Moor Corp.

Saturday they chased balls.

Molly brought the balls back.

Max found a bigger ball.

Sunday is a day for rest.

Molly will rest.

Will Max rest, too?

What Did It Say?

Fill in the circles to answer the questions.

1. Which dog hid under the blanket? ○ Max ○ Molly

2. Which dog found the trash? ○ Max ○ Molly

3. Which dog brought the balls back? ○ Max ○ Molly

4. Which dog buried a bone? ○ Max ○ Molly

5. Which dog popped a balloon? ○ Max ○ Molly

6. Which dog picked some flowers? ○ Max ○ Molly

7. Which dog do you think will try
   to open the gifts? ○ Max ○ Molly

8. Which dog is easier to care for? ○ Max ○ Molly

Max Learns the Hard Way

Color, cut, and paste. Put the pictures in order to tell Max's story.

1

paste

2

paste

3

paste

4

paste

Trouble!

It's easy for Max to get in trouble. Put a check by the things that would mean trouble.

☐ Max chewed the shoe.

☐ Max drank his water.

☐ Max jumped over the gate.

☐ Max chewed on the bone.

☐ Max knocked over the lamp.

☐ Max picked some flowers.

☐ Max took a nap.

☐ Max opened the gifts.

Think about what Max might do next.
Write it here.

_____

Will it mean trouble for Max?   yes   no

Working with Word Families

one

b + one = __ __ __ __   c + one = __ __ __ __

ph + one = __ __ __ __ __   st + one = __ __ __ __ __

thr + one = __ __ __ __ __ __   z + one = __ __ __ __

Write the words to label the pictures.

__ __ __ __ __

__ __ __ __

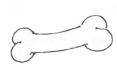

__ __ __ __

__ __ __ __ __ __

end __ __ __ __

What's at the End?

Write the letter that stands for the sound you hear at the end of each word.

do__   doo__

ba__   boo__

cu__   ja__

tu__   ma__

ca__   bo__

Draw a Pup

Follow the steps to draw a puppy.

How is the pup like Max?

_____

How is the pup different from Max?

_____

New Friends

Cookie lived with Amy. She had a dish for water. She had a dish for food. She had a purple mouse with a long tail. She had all that she needed. Cookie loved her home.

One day Amy came home. She had a surprise for Cookie. It was not a new mouse. It was not a new dish. It was a new friend. It was a little gray kitten.

Cookie didn't need a new friend. Cookie ran from Amy. She hid behind the chair.

The new kitten sniffed Cookie's dish. Cookie hissed at the kitten.

The new kitten tasted Cookie's water. Cookie swatted at the kitten.

The new kitten batted Cookie's mouse. Cookie chased the kitten away.

The new kitten cried. It was afraid. Cookie looked at the kitten. It was shaking.

Cookie touched the kitten with her paw. The kitten was soft. Cookie licked the kitten's ear. She licked the kitten's face. The little kitten began to purr.

Cookie didn't need a friend. But the new kitten did. Maybe Cookie could be the new kitten's friend.

Cookie sat on Amy's lap. The little kitten sat next to Cookie. Cookie purred. The little kitten purred.

Cookie played with her mouse. The little kitten played, too.

Cookie curled up for a nap. The little kitten slept. The little kitten had a new friend. Cookie had a new friend, too.

What Did It Say?

Answer each question.
Fill in the circle to mark yes or no.

1. In the beginning Cookie had:

   a dish for water .... ○ yes   ○ no

   a purple bed .... ○ yes   ○ no

   a dish for food .... ○ yes   ○ no

   a yellow mouse .... ○ yes   ○ no

2. Was Cookie happy to see
   Amy's surprise? .... ○ yes   ○ no

3. Cookie

   hissed at the new kitten .... ○ yes   ○ no

   scratched the new kitten .... ○ yes   ○ no

   swatted at the new kitten . ... ○ yes   ○ no

   chased the new kitten................. ○ yes   ○ no

4. The new kitten was afraid. .... ○ yes   ○ no

5. Cookie decided to be the new
   kitten's friend. .... ○ yes   ○ no

What Does It Mean?

Look at the pictures. Write the best word in each sentence.

sniffed	tasted	cried
licked	chased	swatted
purred	played	hissed

The kitten _____ the flower.

Cookie _____ at the kitten.

Cookie _____ the kitten.

The little kitten _____.

The kitten _____ with the yarn.

Cookie _____ the kitten's ear.

Animal Babies

Cut and paste to match the babies with the parents.
Write the names under the pictures.

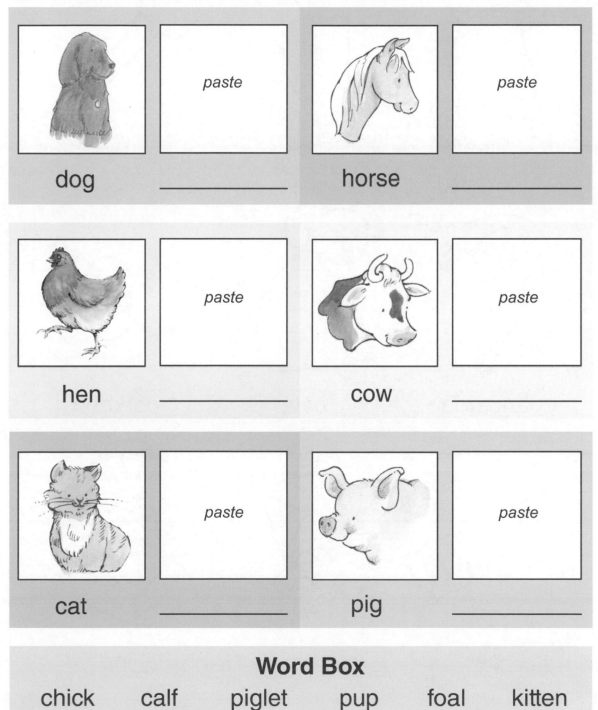

dog _____   paste

horse _____   paste

hen _____   paste

cow _____   paste

cat _____   paste

pig _____   paste

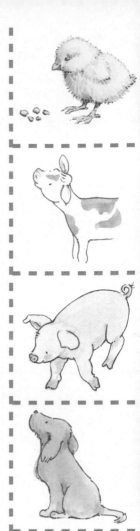

Word Box

chick   calf   piglet   pup   foal   kitten

The Sound of k

Say the picture name. Write the letter **k** where you hear its sound.

__itten __ook __ey

__angaroo __oala __oorknob

__aw __ite __ing

Working with Word Families

ace

f + ace = __ __ __ __

l + ace = __ __ __ __

r + ace = __ __ __ __

pl + ace = __ __ __ __ __

sp + ace = __ __ __ __ __

tr + ace = __ __ __ __ __

Finish each picture. The words tell you what to do.

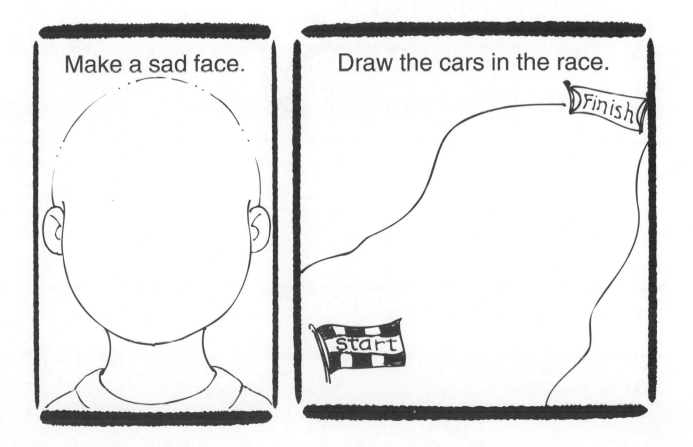

Make a sad face.

Draw the cars in the race.

What Do You Think?

Fill in the circle in front of yes or no.

Can two cats be friends? ○ yes ○ no

Can two cats drive to the mall? ○ yes ○ no

Can two cats like the same toy? ○ yes ○ no

Can two cats chase one another? ○ yes ○ no

Can two cats lap the milk? ○ yes ○ no

Can two cats write a letter? ○ yes ○ no

Draw something two cats could really do.

The Missing Mitten

One day Tommy got ready to go outside. It was a cold, snowy day. Tommy put on his snow pants. He put on his jacket. He put on his long green stocking hat. His mother gave him a scarf to keep his neck warm. Next he pulled on his shiny yellow snow boots. They were new. Tommy couldn't wait to try them out. He was almost ready. All that he needed were his mittens.

Tommy reached into his jacket pocket. He pulled out
one fuzzy blue mitten. One mitten? Where was the other
mitten? Tommy looked all over. He looked like a
marshmallow man stumbling around his room. Where
was the missing mitten?

Tommy yelled to his mom, "Hey, Mom! I can only find
one blue mitten. Will you help me find the other one?"

Tommy's mom came into his room. She took one look at Tommy and started to laugh.

Tommy frowned. "What are you laughing at?" he asked.

Tommy's mom pulled Tommy in front of the mirror. She pointed to his long stocking hat. Peeking out from under the hat was a blue thumb. A hat with a blue thumb?

Tommy reached up and pulled off the hat. There was the missing mitten!

What Did It Say?

Fill in the circle or write words to answer the questions.

1. What was missing?
   ○ hat   ○ scarf   ○ mitten

2. Who did the missing thing belong to?
   ○ Mom   ○ Tommy   ○ Dad

3. Where was the missing thing found?

_____

Draw something that belongs to you that was missing.

Put It in Order

Color, cut, and paste. Show the order that Tommy put on his things before he went outside.

1 — paste

2 — paste

3 — paste

4 — paste

5 — paste

6 — paste

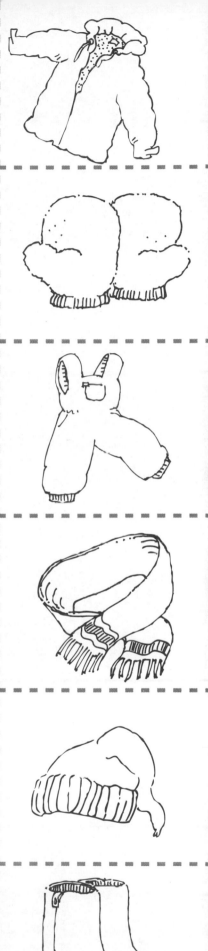

Whose Mittens?

Read the sentences. Then label the mittens.
Use **'s** after the name of the owner.

Tommy has fuzzy blue mittens.

Molly has red mittens with blue stripes.

Baby has mittens with dog ears on them.

Dad has big mittens with metal clips.

__Molly's_____ mittens

_____ mittens

_____ mittens

_____ mittens

Working with Word Families

itten

Write the letters to make new words.

m + itten = __ __ __ __ __ __

k + itten = __ __ __ __ __ __

b + itten = __ __ __ __ __ __

wr + itten = __ __ __ __ __ __ __

Use the new words to complete these sentences.

1. The dog was _____ by a flea.

2. My name is _____ in this book.

3. The _____ has soft fur and a nice meow.

4. The _____ keeps my hand warm when it's cold.

Make Them the Same

Color the second mitten to match the first.
List three words that tell about the mittens.

1. _____

2. _____

3. _____

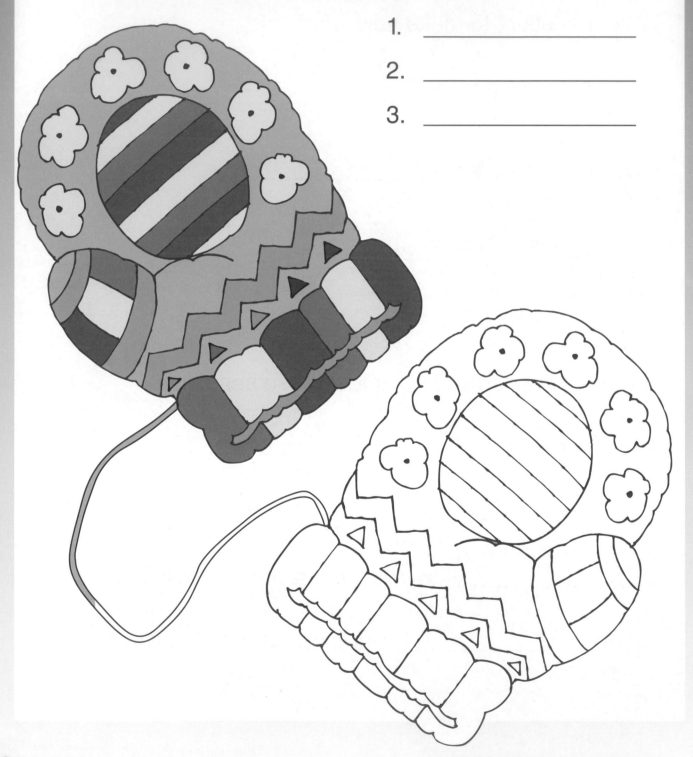

Color Crossword

Use color words to fill in the blanks of this crossword.

Across

3. What color is grape juice and an eggplant?
5. What color is the sky on a sunny day?
7. What color is soot from a fire?
8. What color are ripe tomatoes?
9. What color is the snow?
10. What color is hot chocolate?

Down

1. What color is a ripe pumpkin?
2. What color is a lemon?
3. What color is a cat's tongue?
4. What color is made from black and white?
6. What color is spinach?

black
blue
brown
gray
green
orange
pink
purple
red
white
yellow

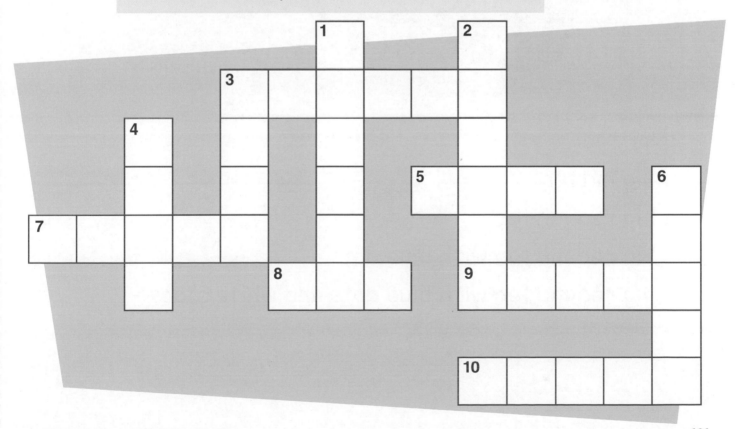

A Mitten

Practice this page until you can read it with no mistakes.
Read it to an adult.

a mitten

a big mitten

a big red mitten

a big red mitten with blue dots

a big red mitten with blue dots and white stars

A New Neighbor

Peter looked down from his window. There was a big moving van next door. He watched as the man unloaded the van.

Peter wanted a new friend—a new friend who could play ball, ride bikes, and build things. Peter watched. The man unloded a bike, a wagon, and a big bear.

Peter smiled. the new family must have a boy.

Just then a car pulled in behind the moving van. It was the new family. Peter watched. The family got out of the car. There was a boy! He had on a blue ball cap. Peter cheered. He watched the new family go inside their house.

Reading • EMC 4529 • © Evan-Moor Corp.

Peter ran downstairs. He grabbed his ball and mitt. He ran next door. He knocked on the door. A man opened the door. Peter said, "Hi, I'm Peter. I live next door. Can your kid come out and play ball?"

The man smiled and said, "I'm glad to meet you, Peter. Sam was hoping to meet a new ball-playing friend. Sam loves to play ball. Sam can catch any ball you throw.

Peter smailed. He couldn't wait to meet Sam. It would be fun to have a pal next door.

The man called, "Sam, come meet our new neighbor. This is Peter. Peter, this is Samantha. We call her Sam."

Peter gulped. Samantha? That was a girl's name. His new neighbor was a girl! The kid with the blue ball cap was a girl? Peter didn't know what to do. He wanted a new friend. He wanted a pal who could play ball. He had thought that pal would be a boy.

Sam smiled at Peter. "Hi, Peter, want to play some catch?"

Peter nodded. He wondered if Sam could really catch. Her dad said she could catch anything.

Later Peter and Sam drank milk and ate cookies. Peter shook his head and smiled. "Sam, your dad was right. You can catch anything I throw. And you throw a mean fast ball, too. I'm glad that you moved next door to me."

After You Read

Practice pages 116 and 117. Use a different voice for each person that is talking. Read the pages to an adult.

What Did It Say?

Fill in the circle to show the answer.

1. How did Peter feel when he met Sam?
   ○ surprised   ○ happy   ○ mad

2. How did Peter feel after he played ball with Sam?
   ○ sad   ○ glad   ○ upset

3. Why did Peter think a new boy had moved in next door?
   ○ The mailman brought a letter.
   ○ His mother told him.
   ○ The moving man unloaded a bike and a wagon.

4. Why did Peter think that the new "boy" liked to play ball?
   ○ The new kid was holding a suitcase.
   ○ The moving man unloaded some bats.
   ○ The new kid was wearing a blue ball cap.

5. What did the new kid's dad boast?
   ○ He said that Sam was a good hitter.
   ○ He said that Sam was a good pitcher.
   ○ He said that Sam could catch any ball Peter threw.

Baseball Words

Use the words below to label the drawing.

baseball	mitt	ball cap	cleats
home plate	bat	backstop	batting glove

The Sound of gr

Color the pictures whose names begin with the sound that **gr** stands for.

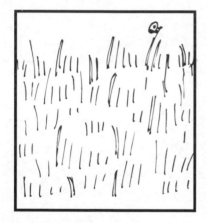

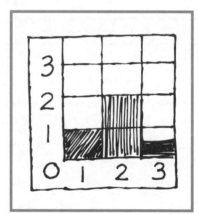

What grade are you in? _____

Is the grass green? _____

Are you ever grumpy? _____

Draw a Story

Cut and paste the sentences in order. Then draw the story.

1

paste

2

paste

3

paste

4

paste

The ball was thrown.

Billy hit the ball hard.

Billy came to the plate.

It was a home run.

Working with Word Families

ay

d + ay = __ __ __   h + ay = __ __ __

cl + ay = __ __ __ __   pl + ay = __ __ __ __

spr + ay = __ __ __ __ __   str + ay = __ __ __ __ __

Use the new words to complete these sentences.

1. The frog is made of _____.

2. The cow sleeps on the _____.

3. I want to go out and _____.

4. _____ the water on the flowers.

5. It's a bright sunny _____.

6. That pup looks like a _____.

George Washington's Barn

George Washington was an important man. Most people know him because he was the first president. Others, because he was a brave soldier.

But George Washington was an important farmer, too. He had a big farm in Virginia. He studied farming. He learned the best way to plant crops. He also learned the best way to harvest crops.

One of the crops that Mr. Washington planted was wheat. Kernels of wheat grow on stalks. When the wheat is ripe, the stalks are cut. The kernels are taken off the stalk. That's a hard job. The stalks are used as straw. The kernels are ground for making bread.

Mr. Washington had a plan. He wanted to make getting the wheat kernels easier. He built a special barn. The barn had 16 sides. It had a ramp up to the door. It was built on a hill so that it had a basement.

Workers cut the wheat. Then they spread it on the floor of the barn. Two mules walked up the ramp into the barn. They walked around and around on the wheat. The kernels of wheat came off the stalks. The kernels fell through holes in the floor to the basement. In the basement, workers swept up the wheat.

George Washington's plan worked. The mules did a good, fast job. The workers were happy. Mr. Washington's wheat was ready for grinding. They could all have bread for dinner!

Reading • EMC 4529 • © Evan-Moor Corp.

What Did It Say?

Think about what you read. Choose the best answer for each question. Look at the story again if you need to.

1. Why do most people know George Washington?
   - ○ He was a brave soldier.
   - ○ He was the first U.S. president.
   - ○ He was a good farmer.

2. Where was George Washington's farm?
   - ○ Washington, D.C.
   - ○ New York
   - ○ Virginia

3. How do you know farming was important to Mr. Washington?
   - ○ He liked to eat bread.
   - ○ He wanted to learn the best way to farm.
   - ○ He fought in a war.

4. Why did Mr. Washington's barn make harvesting wheat easier?
   - ○ It had a ramp so the workers didn't have to go up steps.
   - ○ The mules did most of the work.
   - ○ The workers didn't have to worry about rain.

What Does It Mean?

Read the information below. Use what you learn to fill in the blanks.

George Washington used five different kinds of fences on his farms.

- The **split rail fence** was a moveable fence. It could be laid in a zigzag pattern around trees.

- The **post and rail fence** was a permanent fence. It was used to make boundary lines.

- The **hurdle fence** was a small moveable fence. It was used to keep animals in an area for grazing.

- The **waddle fence** was a tightly woven split rail fence. It was used to pen birds and small animals.

- The **living hedge** was made of bushes. It was used between fields and pastures.

A split rail fence

Write the name of the fence that would be best.

1. A fence between your property and your neighbor's property _____

2. A fence around the chicken yard _____

3. A fence along a border with rocks and trees _____

4. A fence to keep the sheep in one area of the pasture _____

Reading a Map

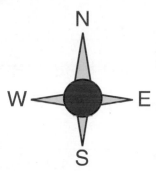

George Washington's big farm was called a plantation. This is a map of his plantation.

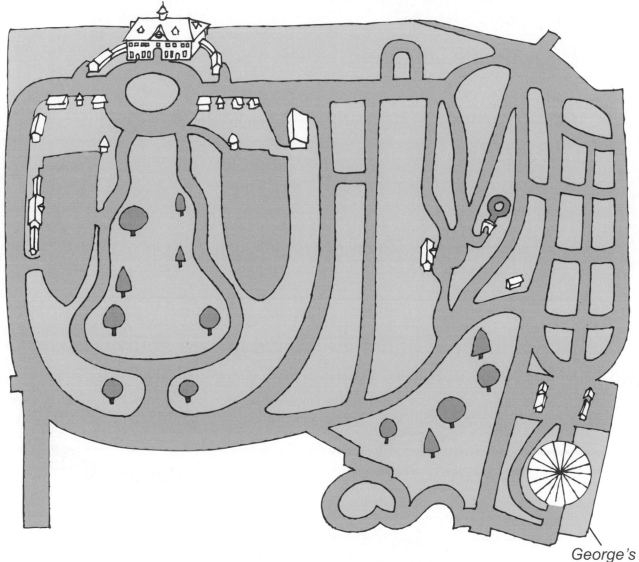

George's barn

Draw a line that shows how George might walk on pathways from his house to his barn.

In which directions would he have to go? _____

The Sounds of ea

The letters **ea** can stand for different sounds. Read the words and listen for two different **ea** sounds.

I am <u>ready</u> to plant the seeds.

<u>Please</u> take your <u>seat</u>.

She fixed the button with a needle and <u>thread</u>.

Put the hat on your <u>head</u>.

Mrs. White gave <u>each</u> of us a <u>treat</u>.

The words that are underlined have the **ea** sound you hear in **bread** or in **wheat**. Write each word in the column where it belongs.

bread

_____

_____

_____

_____

wheat

_____

_____

_____

_____

Put the Steps in Order

Cut and paste.

paste

paste

paste

paste

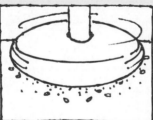

paste

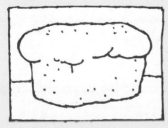

paste

Make some bread.

Plant the wheat seeds.

Take the kernels off the stalk.

Water the seeds.

Cut the wheat stalks.

Grind the kernels into flour.

Working with Word Families

alk

w + alk = __ __ __ __   st + alk = __ __ __ __ __

t + alk = __ __ __ __   ch + alk = __ __ __ __ __

Draw something you would see on a **walk** by a lake.

Draw a place where you cannot **talk**.

Puzzle Page

Cut out the puzzle pieces. Put them together.

What do you have? _____

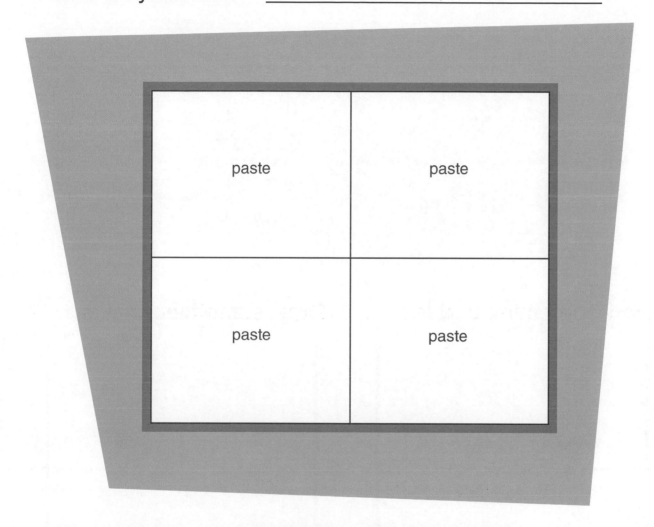

Match the Opposites

Draw a line to match each pair of opposites.

plant	down
hard	slow
fast	harvest
up	less
more	easy

Draw something that is fast.

Draw something that is slow.

Tracking Form

Topic	Color in each page you complete.					
Dad and I	6	7	8	9	10	11
My Cocoon	14	15	16	17	18	19
Who Can Fix It?	24	25	26	27	28	29
Giant Tortoise	31	32	33	34	35	
Put It in the Pack	40	41	42	43		
An Ant on the Rug	48	49	50	51	52	
Who Lives in the Barn?	59	60	61	62	63	64
The Fix-It Man	70	71	72	73	74	75
What a Week!	78	79	80	81	82	83
Molly and Max	88	89	90	91	92	93
New Friends	97	98	99	100	101	102
The Missing Mitten	106	107	108	109	110	111
	112					
A New Neighbor	118	119	120	121	122	
George Washington's Barn	125	126	127	128	129	130
	131	132				

Answer Key

Checking your child's work is an important part of learning. It allows you to see what your child knows well and what areas need more practice. It also provides an opportunity for you to help your child understand that making mistakes is a part of learning.

When an error is discovered, ask your child to look carefully at the question or problem. Errors often occur through misreading. Your child can quickly correct these errors. Help your child with items she or he finds difficult.

The answer key pages can be used in several ways:

- Remove the answer pages and give the book to your child. Go over the answers as each story and the accompanying activity pages are completed.

- Leave the answer pages in the book and give the practice pages to your child one story unit at a time.

Page 6

Page 7

Page 8

Page 9

Page 10

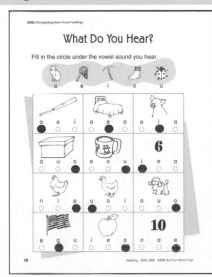

Page 11

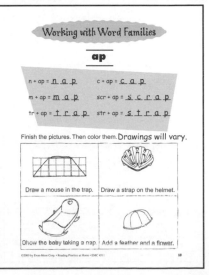

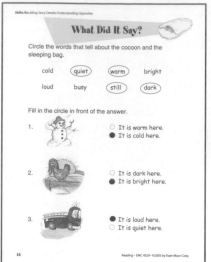

Skills: Recalling Story Details; Understanding Opposites

What Did It Say?

Circle the words that tell about the cocoon and the sleeping bag.

cold   (quiet)   (warm)   bright

loud   busy   (still)   (dark)

Fill in the circle in front of the answer.

1. ○ It is warm here.
   ● It is cold here.

2. ○ It is dark here.
   ● It is bright here.

3. ● It is loud here.
   ○ It is quiet here.

14   Reading • EMC 4529 • ©2005 by Evan-Moor Corp.

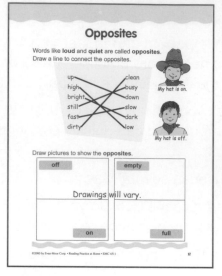

Opposites

Words like **loud** and **quiet** are called **opposites**. Draw a line to connect the opposites.

up — clean
high — busy
bright — down
still — slow
fast — dark
dirty — low

My hat is on.
My hat is off.

Draw pictures to show the **opposites**.

off	empty
Drawings will vary.	
on	full

©2000 by Evan-Moor Corp. • Reading Practice at Home • EMC 4511   17

Real or Make-Believe?

Circle real or make-believe.

real / make-believe ▶
real / make-believe ▶
real / make-believe ◀
real / make-believe ◀

Draw something about a butterfly that could be real.

Draw something about a butterfly that is make-believe.

Drawings will vary.

16   ©2000 by Evan-Moor Corp. • Reading Practice at Home • EMC 4511

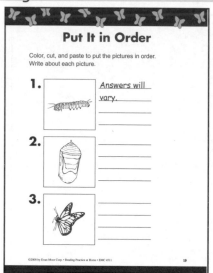

Put It in Order

Color, cut, and paste to put the pictures in order. Write about each picture.

1.   Answers will vary.

2.

3.

©2000 by Evan-Moor Corp. • Reading Practice at Home • EMC 4511   19

Working with Word Families

ill

h + ill = h i l l
f + ill = f i l l
ch + ill = c h i l l
dr + ill = d r i l l

Use the new words to complete these sentences.

1. Please _____ fill _____ my glass with milk.

2. I need a _____ drill _____ to fix the door.

3. He lives at the top of the _____ hill _____

4. If you go out in the cold you will get a _____ chill _____ .

58   ©2000 by Evan-Moor Corp. • Reading Practice at Home • EMC 4511

Skills: Seeing the Whole; Writing a Description

Finish the Picture

Draw the other side of the butterfly. Then color the picture.

Write about the butterfly.

My butterfly _____ Responses will vary. _____

©2005 by Evan-Moor Corp. • EMC 4529 • Reading   19

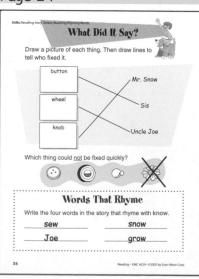

Skills: Recalling Story Details; Matching Rhyming Words

What Did It Say?

Draw a picture of each thing. Then draw lines to tell who fixed it.

button	— Mr. Snow
wheel	— Sis
knob	— Uncle Joe

Which thing could not be fixed quickly?

Words That Rhyme

Write the four words in the story that rhyme with know.

sew   snow

Joe   grow

24   Reading • EMC 4529 • ©2005 by Evan-Moor Corp.

The Same Sound

Color the pictures that begin with the same sound as button.

©2000 by Evan-Moor Corp. • Reading Practice at Home • EMC 4511   27

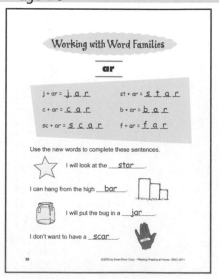

Working with Word Families

ar

j + ar = j a r   st + ar = s t a r
c + ar = c a r   b + ar = b a r
sc + ar = s c a r   f + ar = f a r

Use the new words to complete these sentences.

I will look at the _____ star _____

I can hang from the high _____ bar _____

I will put the bug in a _____ jar _____

I don't want to have a _____ scar _____

28   ©2000 by Evan-Moor Corp. • Reading Practice at Home • EMC 4511

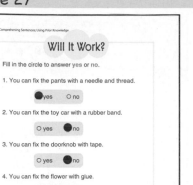

Skills: Comprehending Sentences; Using Prior Knowledge

Will It Work?

Fill in the circle to answer *yes* or *no*.

1. You can fix the pants with a needle and thread.
   ● yes   ○ no

2. You can fix the toy car with a rubber band.
   ○ yes   ● no

3. You can fix the doorknob with tape.
   ○ yes   ● no

4. You can fix the flower with glue.
   ○ yes   ● no

What would you use to fix a cut on your hand?

©2005 by Evan-Moor Corp. • EMC 4529 • Reading   27

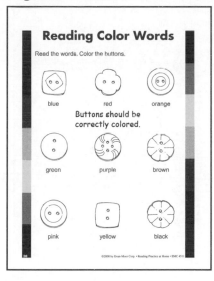

Reading Color Words

Read the words. Color the buttons.

blue   red   orange

Buttons should be correctly colored.

green   purple   brown

pink   yellow   black

©2000 by Evan-Moor Corp. • Reading Practice at Home • EMC 4511

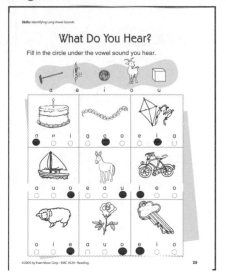

Skills: Identifying Long Vowel Sounds

What Do You Hear?

Fill in the circle under the vowel sound you hear.

©2005 by Evan-Moor Corp. • EMC 4529 • Reading   29

What Did It Say?

1. How does the tortoise move?
   ○ It moves fast.
   ○ It moves quickly.
   ● It moves slowly.

2. What is the tortoise's shell like?
   ○ It's like a tent.
   ● It's like a pack.
   ○ It's like a suitcase.

3. Where does the tortoise walk?
   ○ It walks in the woods.
   ○ It walks in the snow.
   ● It walks in the sand.

Draw a picture of a giant tortoise here.

Drawings will vary.

©2000 by Evan-Moor Corp. • Reading Practice at Home • EMC 4511   33

Working with Word Families

ell

b + ell = b e l l   t + ell = t e l l
sh + ell = s h e l l   w + ell = w e l l
sm + ell = s m e l l   sp + ell = s p e l l

Write one of the new words in each sentence. Then draw a picture to show what the sentence says.

The snail has a hard **shell**

I can **smell** the pretty rose.

Drawings will vary.

The **bell** rings when school starts.

I threw a penny in the wishing **well**

34   ©2000 by Evan-Moor Corp. • Reading Practice at Home • EMC 4511

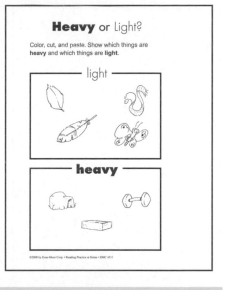

Heavy or Light?

Color, cut, and paste. Show which things are **heavy** and which things are **light**.

light

heavy

©2000 by Evan-Moor Corp. • Reading Practice at Home • EMC 4511

Skills: Following Directions; Writing a Description

Cool, Man, Cool!

The tortoise wants to look cool. Can you color its shell in a special way? Add shoes and a hat.

Tell what the tortoise looks like.
Responses will vary.

34   Reading • EMC 4529 • ©2005 by Evan-Moor Corp.

Skills: Using Prior Knowledge; Completing Sentences

In a Shell

Draw another animal that lives in a shell. Draw the place where it lives, too.

Drawings will vary.

I am a **Responses will vary.**

I live _____

©2005 by Evan-Moor Corp. • Reading   35

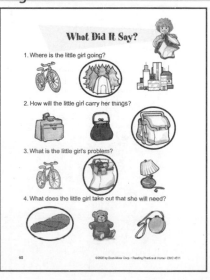

What Did It Say?

1. Where is the little girl going?

2. How will the little girl carry her things?

3. What is the little girl's problem?

4. What does the little girl take out that she will need?

42   ©2000 by Evan-Moor Corp. • Reading Practice at Home • EMC 4511

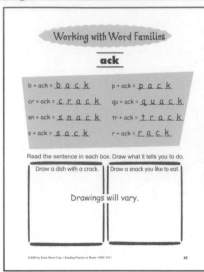

Working with Word Families

ack

b + ack = **b a c k**   p + ack = **p a c k**
cr + ack = **c r a c k**   qu + ack = **q u a c k**
sn + ack = **s n a c k**   tr + ack = **t r a c k**
s + ack = **s a c k**   r + ack = **r a c k**

Read the sentence in each box. Draw what it tells you to do.

Draw a dish with a crack.	Draw a snack you like to eat.
Drawings will vary.	

What Would You Do?

Answer the questions.

What would you do if your pack was too heavy?
■ Take something out.   □ Put something in.

What would you do if it got dark?
□ Turn off the flashlight.   ■ Turn on the flashlight.

What would you do if you got hungry?
■ Eat a snack.   □ Go to bed.

What would you do to stay dry in the rain?
□ Go outside.   ■ Go in the tent.

What would you cook on the fire?
■ Hot dogs and marshmallows   □ Jello and ice cream

Take It Camping!
Circle the things you would take camping.
Draw a line under the ones you would need for school.

Connect the Dots

Start with 1. Make something you might see on a camping trip.

Make a list of animals you might see on a camping trip.
Responses will vary.

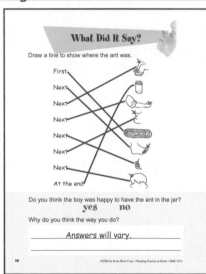

What Did It Say?

Draw a line to show where the ant was.

First
Next
Next
Next
Next
Next
At the end

Do you think the boy was happy to have the ant in the jar?
yes   no

Why do you think the way you do?

Answers will vary.

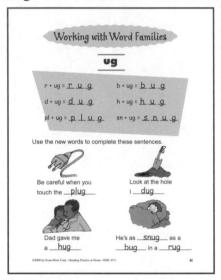

Working with Word Families

ug

r + ug = **r u g**   b + ug = **b u g**
d + ug = **d u g**   h + ug = **h u g**
pl + ug = **p l u g**   sn + ug = **s n u g**

Use the new words to complete these sentences.

Be careful when you touch the **plug**

Look at the hole I **dug**

Dad gave me a **hug**

He's as **snug** as a **bug** in a **rug**

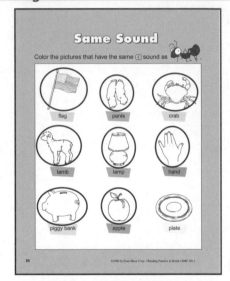

Same Sound

Color the pictures that have the same ă sound as

flag   pants   crab
lamb   lamp   hand
piggy bank   apple   plate

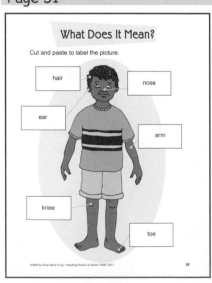

What Does It Mean?

Cut and paste to label the picture.

hair   nose
ear   arm
knee   toe

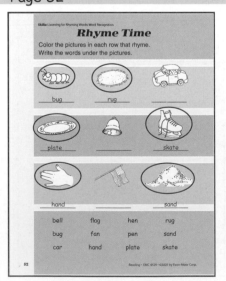

Rhyme Time

Color the pictures in each row that rhyme.
Write the words under the pictures.

bug   rug
plate   skate
hand   sand

bell   flag   hen   rug
bug   fan   pen   sand
car   hand   plate   skate

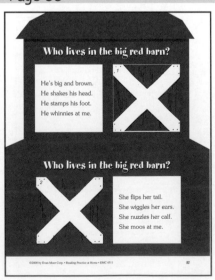

Who lives in the big red barn?

He's big and brown.
He shakes his head.
He stamps his foot.
He whinnies at me.

Who lives in the big red barn?

She flips her tail.
She wiggles her ears.
She nuzzles her calf.
She moos at me.

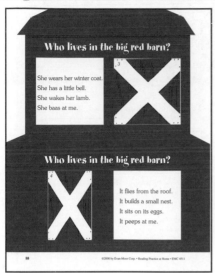

Who lives in the big red barn?

She wears her winter coat.
She has a little bell.
She wakes her lamb.
She baas at me.

Who lives in the big red barn?

It flies from the roof.
It builds a small nest.
It sits on its eggs.
It peeps at me.

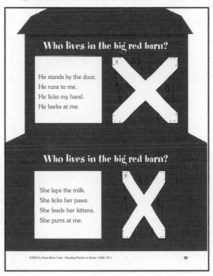

Who lives in the big red barn?

He stands by the door.
He runs to me.
He licks my hand.
He barks at me.

Who lives in the big red barn?

She laps the milk.
She licks her paws.
She feeds her kittens.
She purrs at me.

Who lives in the big red barn?

It runs so fast.
It hides so well.
It nibbles food.
It squeaks at me.

Who lives in the big red barn?

Skills: Recalling Story Details

What Did It Say?

Fill in the circle under the correct answer.

1. Who builds a small nest?
   sheep · **swallow** · cat · mouse

2. Who nibbles food?
   sheep · swallow · cat · **mouse**

3. Who has a lamb?
   sheep · swallow · cat · mouse

4. Who flips her tail?
   horse · **cow** · dog · cat

5. Who licks a paw?
   horse · cow · dog · **cat**

6. Who barks?
   horse · cow · **dog** · cat

7. Who stamps a foot?
   horse · cow · dog · cat

Working with Word Families

ake

c + ake = c a k e   sn + ake = s n a k e
r + ake = r a k e   sh + ake = s h a k e
fl + ake = f l a k e   br + ake = b r a k e

Write the correct -ake word to finish each sentence.
Draw a picture to show what the sentence says.

I _rake_ up the leaves.   A _flake_ of snow is on my nose.

Drawings will vary.

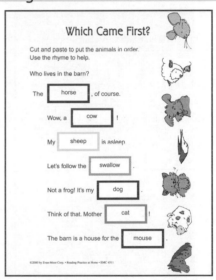

Which Came First?

Cut and paste to put the animals in order.
Use the rhyme to help.

Who lives in the barn?

The [horse], of course.

Wow, a [cow] !

My [sheep] is asleep.

Let's follow the [swallow]

Not a frog! It's my [dog]

Think of that. Mother [cat] !

The barn is a house for the [mouse]

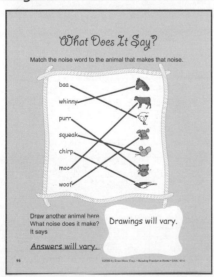

What Does It Say?

Match the noise word to the animal that makes that noise.

baa
whinny
purr
squeak
chirp
moo
woof

Draw another animal here.
What noise does it make?
It says

Answers will vary.

Drawings will vary.

Think About It

Which animals live mainly on a farm?
Which animals live mainly in the jungle?
Write the names of the animals in the correct list.

goat · lion · elephant · chicken
horse · zebra · cow · monkey

On a farm   In the jungle

goat   lion
chicken   elephant
horse   zebra
cow   monkey

The Big Red Barn

The picture should be correctly colored.
Read the color words. Then color the picture.

yellow · green · green · green · red · brown · yellow · black · pink · brown · orange · blue

---

Page 70

What Did It Say?

Fill in the circle by the correct answer.

1. Who did the boy call for help?
   ○ Mother ○ a friend ● Mr. Fix-It

2. What was wrong with the window?
   ○ It was stuck. ● It broke. ○ It needed washing.

3. Was Mr. Fix-It a good fixer?
   ○ No, he had to keep coming back.
   ○ Yes, he won a prize.
   ● Yes, he fixed everything.

4. Why do you think the boy called Mr. Fix-It the last time?
   ○ There were too many cookies in the jar.
   ○ The milk was going to spoil.
   ● Mr. Fix-It should have a treat.

Write an answer.
Who fixes things at your house?

_____Answers will vary._____

©2000 by Evan-Moor Corp. • Reading Practice at Home • EMC 4511

Page 71

Put It in Order

Mr. Fix-It will fix the wagon. Color the pictures.
Cut and paste them in the correct order.

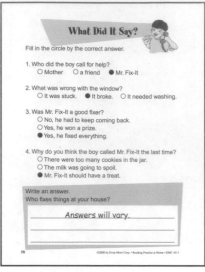

The pictures should be colored.

©2000 by Evan-Moor Corp. • Reading Practice at Home • EMC 4511

Page 72

Can It Be Fixed?

Some things cannot be put back together.
Write It can be fixed or It can't by each of the pictures below. Use your best handwriting.

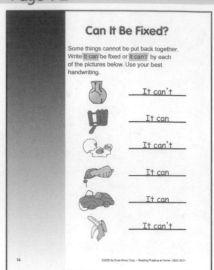

It can't
It can
It can't
It can
It can
It can't

©2000 by Evan-Moor Corp. • Reading Practice at Home • EMC 4511

Page 73

Working with Word Families

ink

p + ink = p i n k   s + ink = s i n k
bl + ink = b l i n k   dr + ink = d r i n k
shr + ink = s h r i n k   th + ink = t h i n k

Draw a toy boat in a sink.	Draw a muddy pig that's pink.
Drawings will vary.	

©2000 by Evan-Moor Corp. • Reading Practice at Home • EMC 4511

Page 74

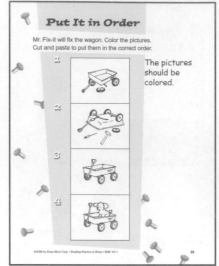

More Than One

Add s to each word to mean more than one.
Then draw what the words say.

one door
two doors

one house
three houses

Drawings will vary.

one bird
four birds

one flower
five flowers

©2000 by Evan-Moor Corp. • Reading Practice at Home • EMC 4511

Page 75

Rhyme Time

Color the pictures. Circle the words that rhyme.

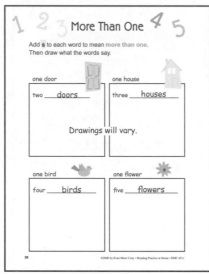

house   mouse   cat
window   sink   ink
door   bear   chair
dish   milk   fish
cake   snake   hat

©2000 by Evan-Moor Corp. • Reading Practice at Home • EMC 4511

Page 78

Skills: Recalling Story Details

What Did I Have?

Fill in the circle under of the correct answer.

1. What did I have on Tuesday?
   turkey   tuna   soup

2. What did I have on Friday?
   waffles   muffins   fries

3. What did I have on Sunday?
   soup   soda   turkey

4. What did I have on Monday?
   waffles   fries   muffins

5. What did I have on Saturday?
   soup   soda   tuna

Reading • EMC 4529 • ©2005 by Evan-Moor Corp.

Page 79

My Favorite Foods

Rewrite the story. Draw or write what you would like to eat each day beside the name of the day. Then read the story using your foods.

Monday I have	Answers will vary.
Tuesday I have	
Wednesday I have	
Thursday I have	
Friday I have	
Saturday I have	
Sunday I have	

©2000 by Evan-Moor Corp. • Reading Practice at Home • EMC 4511

Page 80

Working with Word Families

unch

l + unch = l u n c h   m + unch = m u n c h
b + unch = b u n c h   p + unch = p u n c h
cr + unch = c r u n c h

Circle each word from the -unch family in the story below.
Draw pictures to show the animals eating.

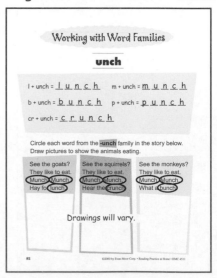

See the goats?
They like to eat.
Munch, Munch.
Hay for lunch.

See the squirrels?
They like to eat.
Munch, Munch.
Hear the crunch.

See the monkeys?
They like to eat.
Munch, Munch.
What a bunch.

Drawings will vary.

©2000 by Evan-Moor Corp. • Reading Practice at Home • EMC 4511

Page 81

Noisy Foods

Some foods are noisy. Color the things that make crunchy noises when you eat them. Write **munch** under the ones you like to eat.

Answers will vary.

Page 82

How Does It Taste?

Write one letter of the food name in each box. When all the boxes have been filled in, read the secret message in the pink boxes.

Foods		
milk	apple	custard
fruit	cookie	bread
eggs	chocolate	pudding

c u s t a r d
b r e a d
a p p l e
f r u i t
c o o k i e
m i l k
c h o c o l a t e
p u d d i n g
e g g s

Write the secret message here: __delicious__

Page 83

Food Word Search

See how many of the foods in the Word Box you can find.

Word Box		
☑ apple	☑ banana	☑ spaghetti
☑ cookie	☑ pizza	☑ cheese
☑ grapes	☑ pancake	☑ hamburger
☑ orange	☑ carrot	☑ tuna
☑ potatoes	☑ eggs	☑ corn

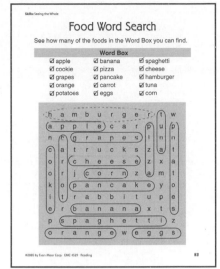

Page 88

What Did It Say?

Fill in the circles to answer the questions.

1. Which dog hid under the blanket? ○ Max ● Molly
2. Which dog found the trash? ● Max ○ Molly
3. Which dog brought the balls back? ○ Max ● Molly
4. Which dog buried a bone? ○ Max ● Molly
5. Which dog popped a balloon? ● Max ○ Molly
6. Which dog picked some flowers? ● Max ○ Molly
7. Which dog do you think will try to open the gifts? ● Max ○ Molly
8. Which dog is easier to care for? ○ Max ● Molly

Page 89

Max Learns the Hard Way

Color, cut, and paste. Put the pictures in order to tell Max's story.

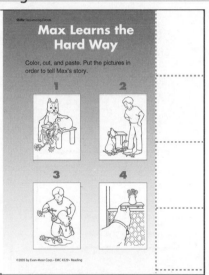

Page 90

Trouble!

It's easy for Max to get in trouble. Put a check by the things that would mean **trouble**.

☑ Max chewed the shoe.
☐ Max drank his water.
☑ Max jumped over the gate.
☐ Max chewed on the bone.
☑ Max knocked over the lamp.
☑ Max picked some flowers.
☐ Max took a nap.
☑ Max opened the gifts.

Think about what Max might do next. Write it here.

___Answers will vary.___

Will it mean trouble for Max?   yes   no

Page 91

Working with Word Families

one

b + one = __b o n e__   c + one = __c o n e__

ph + one = __p h o n e__   st + one = __s t o n e__

thr + one = __t h r o n e__   z + one = __z o n e__

Write the words to label the pictures.

__p h o n e__   __c o n e__

__t h r o n e__   __b o n e__

__s t o n e__   end __z o n e__

Page 92

What's at the End?

Write the letter that stands for the sound you hear at the end of each word.

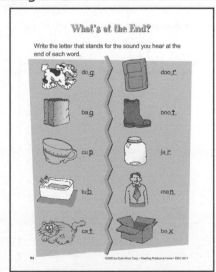

do __g__   doo __r__

ba __g__   boo __t__

cu __p__   ja __r__

tu __b__   ma __n__

ca __t__   bo __x__

Page 93

Draw a Pup

Follow the steps to draw a puppy.

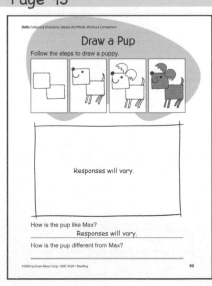

Responses will vary.

How is the pup like Max?
___Responses will vary.___

How is the pup different from Max?

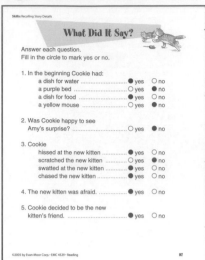

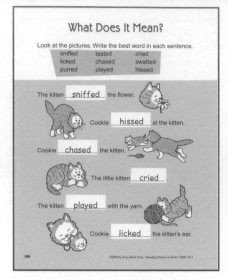

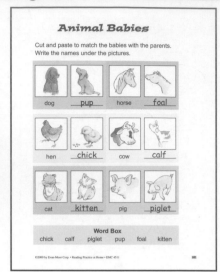

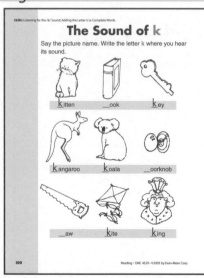

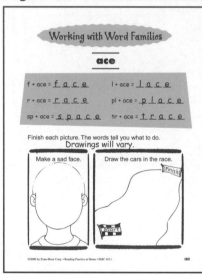

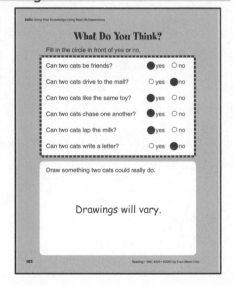

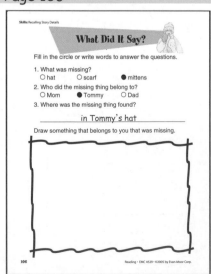

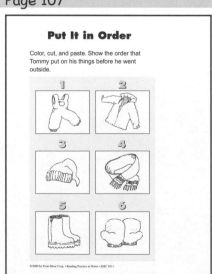

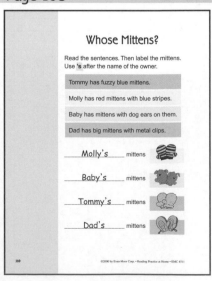

Page 109

Page 109

Working with Word Families

itten

Write the letters to make new words.

m + itten = m i t t e n

k + itten = k i t t e n

b + itten = b i t t e n

wr + itten = w r i t t e n

Use the new words to complete these sentences.

1. The dog was __bitten__ by a flea.

2. My name is __written__ in this book.

3. The __kitten__ has soft fur and a nice meow.

4. The __mitten__ keeps my hand warm when it's cold.

©2000 by Evan-Moor Corp. • Reading Practice at Home • EMC 4511   111

Page 110

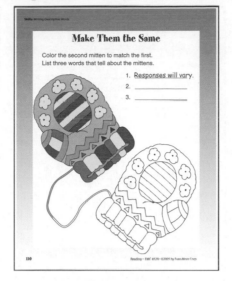

Skills: Writing Descriptive Words

Make Them the Same

Color the second mitten to match the first.
List three words that tell about the mittens.

1. __Responses will vary.__
2. _____
3. _____

110   Reading • EMC 4529 • ©2005 by Evan-Moor Corp.

Page 111

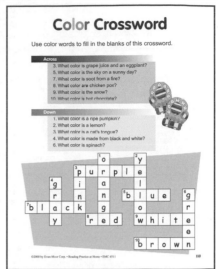

Color Crossword

Use color words to fill in the blanks of this crossword.

Across

3. What color is grape juice and an eggplant?
5. What color is the sky on a sunny day?
7. What color is soot from a fire?
8. What color are chicken pox?
9. What color is the snow?
10. What color is hot chocolate?

Down

1. What color is a ripe pumpkin?
2. What color is a lemon?
3. What color is a cat's tongue?
4. What color is made from black and white?
6. What color is spinach?

Crossword answers:
- purple
- orange
- yellow
- pink
- gray
- green
- black
- red
- blue
- white
- brown

©2000 by Evan-Moor Corp. • Reading Practice at Home • EMC 4511   111

Page 112

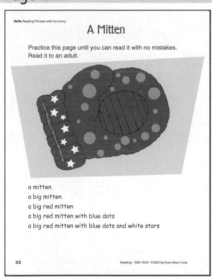

Skills: Reading Phrases with Accuracy

A Mitten

Practice this page until you can read it with no mistakes.
Read it to an adult.

a mitten
a big mitten
a big red mitten
a big red mitten with blue dots
a big red mitten with blue dots and white stars

112   Reading • EMC 4529 • ©2005 by Evan-Moor Corp.

Page 118

What Did It Say?

1. How did Peter feel when he met Sam?
   ☒ surprised ☐ happy ☐ mad

2. How did Peter feel after he played ball with Sam?
   ☐ sad ☒ glad ☐ upset

3. Why did Peter think a new boy had moved in next door?
   ☐ The mailman brought a letter.
   ☐ His mother told him.
   ☒ The moving man unloaded a bike and a wagon.

4. Why did Peter think that the new "boy" liked to play ball?
   ☐ The new kid was holding a suitcase.
   ☐ The moving man unloaded some bats.
   ☒ The new kid was wearing a blue ball cap.

5. What did the new kid's dad boast?
   ☐ He said that Sam was a good hitter.
   ☐ He said that Sam was a good pitcher.
   ☒ He said that Sam could catch any ball Peter threw.

118   ©2000 by Evan-Moor Corp. • Reading Practice at Home • EMC 4511

Page 119

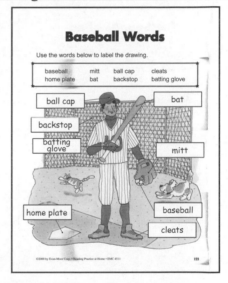

Baseball Words

Use the words below to label the drawing.

| baseball | mitt | ball cap | cleats |
| home plate | bat | backstop | batting glove |

Labels: ball cap, bat, backstop, batting glove, mitt, home plate, baseball, cleats

©2000 by Evan-Moor Corp. • Reading Practice at Home • EMC 4511   119

Page 120

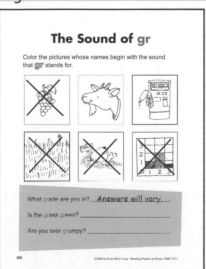

The Sound of gr

Color the pictures whose names begin with the sound that **gr** stands for.

What grade are you in? __Answers will vary.__

Is the grass green? _____

Are you ever grumpy? _____

120   ©2000 by Evan-Moor Corp. • Reading Practice at Home • EMC 4511

Page 121

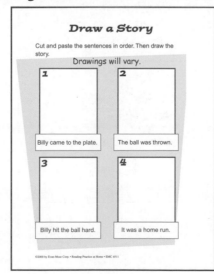

Draw a Story

Cut and paste the sentences in order. Then draw the story.

__Drawings will vary.__

1
2
3
4

Billy came to the plate.
The ball was thrown.
Billy hit the ball hard.
It was a home run.

©2000 by Evan-Moor Corp. • Reading Practice at Home • EMC 4511

Page 122

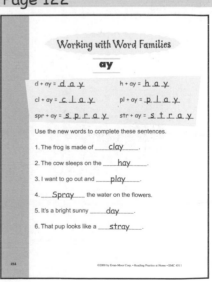

Working with Word Families

ay

d + ay = d a y   h + ay = h a y

cl + ay = c l a y   pl + ay = p l a y

spr + ay = s p r a y   str + ay = s t r a y

Use the new words to complete these sentences.

1. The frog is made of __clay__.

2. The cow sleeps on the __hay__.

3. I want to go out and __play__.

4. __Spray__ the water on the flowers.

5. It's a bright sunny __day__.

6. That pup looks like a __stray__.

124   ©2000 by Evan-Moor Corp. • Reading Practice at Home • EMC 4511

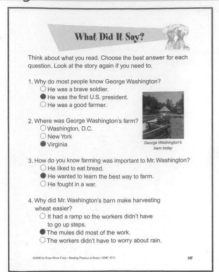

What Did It Say?

Think about what you read. Choose the best answer for each question. Look at the story again if you need to.

1. Why do most people know George Washington?
   - ○ He was a brave soldier.
   - ● He was the first U.S. president.
   - ○ He was a good farmer.

2. Where was George Washington's farm?
   - ○ Washington, D.C.
   - ○ New York
   - ● Virginia

George Washington's barn today

3. How do you know farming was important to Mr. Washington?
   - ○ He liked to eat bread.
   - ● He wanted to learn the best way to farm.
   - ○ He fought in a war.

4. Why did Mr. Washington's barn make harvesting wheat easier?
   - ○ It had a ramp so the workers didn't have to go up steps.
   - ● The mules did most of the work.
   - ○ The workers didn't have to worry about rain.

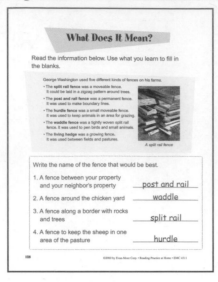

What Does It Mean?

Read the information below. Use what you learn to fill in the blanks.

George Washington used five different kinds of fences on his farms.
- The **split rail fence** was a moveable fence. It could be laid in a zigzag pattern around trees.
- The **post and rail fence** was a permanent fence. It was used to mark boundary lines.
- The **hurdle fence** was a small moveable fence. It was used to keep animals in an area for grazing.
- The **waddle fence** was a tightly woven split rail fence. It was used to pen birds and small animals.
- The **living hedge** was a growing fence. It was used between fields and pastures.

A split rail fence

Write the name of the fence that would be best.

1. A fence between your property and your neighbor's property .... post and rail
2. A fence around the chicken yard .... waddle
3. A fence along a border with rocks and trees .... split rail
4. A fence to keep the sheep in one area of the pasture .... hurdle

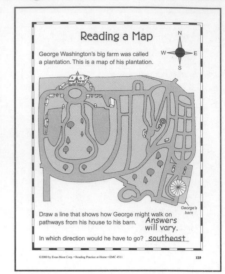

Reading a Map

George Washington's big farm was called a plantation. This is a map of his plantation.

George's barn

Draw a line that shows how George might walk on pathways from his house to his barn. Answers will vary.

In which direction would he have to go? southeast

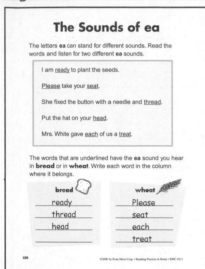

The Sounds of ea

The letters **ea** can stand for different sounds. Read the words and listen for two different **ea** sounds.

I am <u>ready</u> to plant the seeds.

<u>Please</u> take your seat.

She fixed the button with a needle and <u>thread</u>.

Put the hat on your <u>head</u>.

Mrs. White gave <u>each</u> of us a <u>treat</u>.

The words that are underlined have the **ea** sound you hear in **bread** or in **wheat**. Write each word in the column where it belongs.

bread	wheat
ready	Please
thread	seat
head	each
	treat

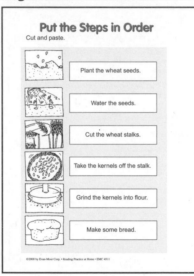

Put the Steps in Order
Cut and paste.

- Plant the wheat seeds.
- Water the seeds.
- Cut the wheat stalks.
- Take the kernels off the stalk.
- Grind the kernels into flour.
- Make some bread.

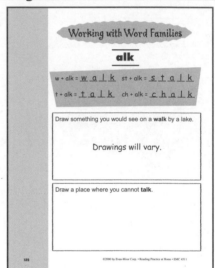

Working with Word Families

alk

w + alk = w a l k   st + alk = s t a l k
t + alk = t a l k   ch + alk = c h a l k

Draw something you would see on a **walk** by a lake.

Drawings will vary.

Draw a place where you cannot **talk**.

Puzzle Page

Cut out the puzzle pieces. Put them together.

What do you have? <u>George Washington's Barn</u>

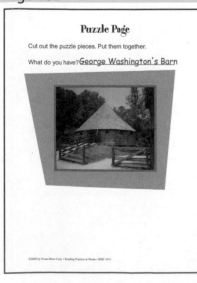

Match the Opposites

Draw a line to match each pair of opposites.

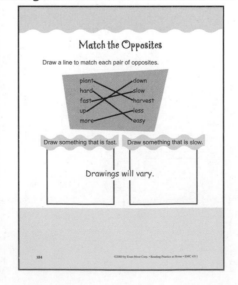

plant — harvest
hard — easy
fast — slow
up — down
more — less

Draw something that is fast. | Draw something that is slow.

Drawings will vary.